On Any Given Day...

A Butterfly Could Be a Blessing!

Carolyn Saunders Banks

Books Academy LLC
112 SW H K Dodgen Loop,
Temple, Texas 76504
Hotline: (254) 800-1189

Ordering Information:
Quantity sales. Special discounts are available on quantity purchases by corporations, associations, and others. For details, contact the publisher at the address above.

Printed in the United States of America.

ISBN-13:	Softcover	978-1-964929-39-2
	Hardcover	978-1-964929-41-5
	eBook	978-1-964929-40-8

Library of Congress Control Number: 2024919426

Dedicated To:

Pastor Donald R. Ingram, Sr.

…who kept pushing

Ms. Katherine C. Whitaker

…who kept asking

Mrs. Linda H. Wilson

…who kept supporting

Ms. Amy P. Harper

…who allowed her creativity to flow

Mrs. Natalie S. Perkins

…who extended her expertise to review

For you, the reader,

may His Grace and Peace

be granted

with

My Sincere Thanks

THE BLESSING

A Different Perspective…

A golden, tangerine bronzed leaf…
Swaying jonquils bright yellow in the sun…
Sheer clouds float effortlessly against a cobalt sky…
The soft sense of a newborn's cheek…each a blessing

The fleeting thought of a memory long past…
A human connection, gentle and meaningful…
A glistening rainbow through wet sunshine…
The sound and smell of fresh fallen snow…each a blessing

The continuous repetitive beat of a heart…
A gentle breeze brushing against one's being…
An unwritten melody sung to God from the heart…
Relaxing the brain to think about nothing…each a blessing

A Gentle Butterfly …A Blessing

THE AUTHOR IS…

C charismatic
  A artistic
    R reasonable
      O organized
        L logical
          Y youth-oriented
          N nocturnal
S sentimental
  A articulate
    U unique perfectionist
      N natural-born cook
        D detailed-oriented
          E extraordinary
          R respectful
            S self-confident
B bold
  A advocate for truth
    N normal (whatever that means)
      K kindhearted
      S sociable

Table of Contents

Black History: Look Back To Appreciate And Learn...

ALLOW ME TO INTRODUCE...
People in Circumstances! More Alike than Different

CELEBRATE
The Joy of Living! Every Day Is a Blessing!

PRAYERS AND RESPONSES
Supplications with Sincerity! Prayer Changes Things!

Foreword

When I initially read her first book, *On Any Given Day…A Butterfly May Cross Your Path*, I did not take the time to carefully ponder the words or their sentiment. I was so excited to read the published writings of my life-long friend that all I wanted to do was read each entry as quickly as possible, so I could let her know I was finished. I was anxious to share with Carolyn, my pride in her accomplishment. I was reading the entries page by page in anticipation of the selection included in this collection that had been specifically written for me. A personal and emotional gift of poetry Carolyn had written, framed, and given to me at the time of the loss of Maika, my eighteen-year-old daughter, a college freshman, and my only child. Carolyn did not mention to me that this particular poem had been included in her book, but as one who reads the Table of Contents before delving into any book, I saw the title as I skimmed the list. I resisted the compelling desire to turn immediately to my poem, "To Mom from Maika"; however, I did use speed-reading skills to scan the selections as quickly as possible until I reached page 44. Here, I lingered, filling my mind, heart, and soul, my very being with these words I had already read countless times before. My gratefulness for the gift of this poem is unending. Seeing it as an inclusion in a completed and published book of writings is truly indescribable, and yes, it is most definitely my favorite.

It took a second reading for me to absorb the meanings, often replete with double entendre, within each piece. Subsequent readings have influenced me to consider more thoughtfully those events occurring in daily life that most of us take for granted. In the first collection of poetry, prose, and thoughts, Carolyn celebrates the memorable, comforts the weary, honors the deserving, and most importantly, thanks the Provider for every single aspect of our lives. Carolyn fulfilled her dream of creating a work through which she could share her thoughts and her heart with family, friends, and readers-at-large, who, upon, either a casual or more reflective reading, will discover a connection on the pages of this nightstand gift, with their own lives. This was the foundation for Book 2.

The publication of *On Any Given Day…A Butterfly May Cross Your Path*, fulfilled Carolyn's dream, but it was only the beginning. Now she continues the realization of that dream by thinking from a different perspective with *On Any Day…A Butterfly Could Be a Blessing!* In Book 2, Carolyn answers the call to distinguish between merely accepting the ordinary or taking the mundane and making it creatively vibrant. Carolyn Saunders Banks has provided a unique way of viewing everyday thinking. She desires that the deliberate and forgotten become the thriving possibilities that are full of positive life. Her goals are to encourage a closer Godly walk and consequently a more fervent relationship with our daily physical, spiritual, and earthly lives. We will continue to grow in our appreciation of life each time we awaken to face another day. After all, regardless of past experiences, this could be a day when a butterfly of hope, joy, or possibility crosses our paths to be a blessing.

Amy M. Harper
Florissant, MO
July 19, 2009

SPIRITUAL SECURITY

HIS PRESENCE IN ALL THINGS!
GOD IS OMNIPOTENT!

GOD CAN MOVE ANY MOUNTAIN

I have a mountain in my face,
For I have fallen far from grace,
Though very small was the stumble,
I still suffered a major tumble.

When the mountain presses hard
Generating thoughts like glassy shards,
An innate signal sounds an alarm,
That unnerves my space and causes harm.

A definite mountain in the distance,
But acknowledgement presents resistance,
Now is the time for solid backing,
Instead a plan seems totally lacking.

Help needed! This battle cannot be won.
What do I do? How do I do it? When should it be done?
Those intrinsic triggers begin to kick in.
For God placed them in me so *He* could defend.
A pause for clarity, for spiritual sight...
A ferocious heartbeat for a mental fight,

Pumping blood to carry the weight,
Of the hurt and trepidation on my plate
Intense eyes are focused and ready…
Conscious awareness, course held steady.

So I look that mountain directly in the "eye."
Letting it know I'm not ready to die.
I make that mountain my focal point,
And wait for God's presence to bless and anoint.

I order my steps with prayer and fasting,
Quiet moments will come, comforting and lasting.
I raise a confident voice to the mountain and say,
"The battle is not mine, no…not this day!"

For God has declared, "No need to battle man.
Stay in my Word and there you must stand.
You cannot see, not that you should,
All that I do works together for good."

There by no means will my problem stay,
I clasp hands together to sincerely pray…
For the Master to fulfill His promised plan,
And move the mountain in whose shadow I stand.

BE STILL AND LISTEN

Our world today is loud and busy. The music, regardless of type: hip-hop, rock, sacred, or gospel seems to bombard us from all directions at unbelievable volumes. Television commercials are recorded dozens of decibels higher than the newscast, documentary, sporting event, or other programming. They scream the deals, the pitches, and the testimonials to get the audience's attention. Because of ongoing hearing losses occurring today, people are shouting at each other to be heard, noticed, or understood.

As we turn the technology up, we are multi-tasking to execute numerous starts of necessary and unnecessary assignments; it is not easy to keep a straight thought, no less hear a still, small voice. What messages are we receiving from all this noise and busyness? What positive points are being poured into our being? With all that we have on our plates, the way we run from task to task, as much time as it takes to manage the lives connected to ours, God is not being heard.

Can we not steal away for a solitary moment to commune with the Master? Time seems to be moving more quickly as our days advance. Tomorrows are not a given expectation. "in his still small voice, he will direct your path, for the words of wise men are heard in quiet, more than the loud cry of a ruler of foolish people" (Ecclesiastes 9:17 paraphrased).

It is the time to "Be Still and Listen." God is trying to tell us something!

GOD GIVES US POSITIVE GLIMPSES

Every day, there are moments that give us a sense of God's
preeminence.
Brilliant Sunrises,
Exceptional Butterflies,
Delicate Songbirds,
Resplendent Flowers,
Unique Rainbows,
Animated Cumulus Clouds,
Glorious Sunsets

Then God gives us a valuable asset from the past to utilize…Seniors
who share…
Warm Smiles,
Sincere Encouragement,
Fond Memories,
Solid Experiences
Esteemed Wisdom
Earned Insight
Wonderful Recipes

Finally, God gives us youth who offer hope for the future with…

Giftedness,
    Skillful Questioning,
        Meaningful Accomplishments,
            Inspired Creativity,
                Dedication to Task,
                    Fearless Ideas,
                        Self-motivated Orations,
                            Unassailable Confidence.

With all these glimpses, the potential for positive prospective
    Abounds.

GOD IS...

God is…a friend with whom you can share your deepest secrets.

God is…a protector who shields you with His hedge of angels.

God is…a companion who will converse with you when loneliness takes over the night.

God is…a comforter who tenderly wraps His arms of love around the sobs of hurt, loss, and despair.

God is…an instructor who has told us exactly how life should be lived.

God is…a forgiver who understands human frailties and grants request for absolution.

God is… *The One* who hears our silent prayers and answers.

God is… *The One* who allows us to embrace a brand-new day each morning.

God is…God! Aren't you glad?

GOD WATCHES OVER

North, south, east, or west, it doesn't matter where you are.

The hand of God can follow you whether here or near or far.

It does not matter whether it's employment, rest, or play,

you are under His protection in every possible way.

The highways can be dangerous, with speed and crazy turns.

At times not knowing how you made it, but lessons were surely learned.

Traverse a street in sunlight or in the middle of the night,

could leave you vulnerable to harsh result, if not for angels' flight.

Planes, trains, or a flight of stairs can initiate a quick demise,

so maintaining heavenly contact seems intelligent and wise.

When something evil comes along, and fear stops you in your tracks,

you wonder what you should have done to have Him watch your back.

If your prayer life's sound and communication is strong,

there's little to fear for nothing can go wrong.

God knows where you are, no need for alarm,

He'll keep you safe and free from harm.

Ignore what you see and trust what you believe.

God is Omnipotent, complete safety you can achieve.

Following the path God laid for your life

will keep you protected with little strife.

KNOWN BY GOD

Prayers and supplications
    Benevolent word
        Angry exchanges
            Expressions of the heart
            All heard by God.

The smallest kindness
    A supportive, loving smile
        Turbulent gestures
            Broken hearts, embarrassments
            All seen by God

The sparrow, the ant
    The newborn, the unborn
        Those who have everything, those who have nothing
            Males, females, those undecided
            All touched by God.

DNA, the Creation,
    The future, infinity,
        Perfection, black holes,

The Bermuda Triangle
All understood by God.

Black, white, green, red
   Tall, short, squatty, lean
      Beauty, handsome, plain, grotesque
         Most educated, graduate, self-taught, dropout
         All loved by God.

9

LIFE IS SO MANY GOOD THINGS

It is far too easy to focus on and complain about the bad experiences
we seem to encounter daily.

But think about all the blessings, miracles, and marvels that also
occur in our lives each day.

Our safe arrivals and returns, (long distances and shorter trips),
communication between family members, friends, and strangers, are
our little miracles.

The thought processes that allow us to remember the how to, the
when and the where, the organ function and interactions within our
bodies are God's authorizations that keep us going and going and
going.

We do none of these on our own. We function because "A loving
Father" made us so perfectly that we can, without winding, shaking,
or being plugged in.

He alone controls our actions and our situations.

So as we arrive safely, snap a finger, wink an eye, bend our toes, curl
our lips to a smile, or put one foot in front of the other…

Think about each simple execution as a blessing that has been
specifically granted to each of us by God.

Remember to be grateful.

UNREMITTING PAIN

Pain…an invasion of privacy.

An area…never a minute spot where the knife pricked or the object bumped or the body part hit.

On occasion, none of these occurred. The reason for onset is undetermined.

Pain births itself…in the center of a thought, a bloody arterial path, or a catacomb of questionable cells.

It makes its presence known with an ache, a piercing dart, a spreading burn, or a pulsating, pounding, continuous beat.

Pain can be felt an unbelievable distance from the offending site, taking the attention of the strongest focus, the steadiest hand, or the most intelligent articulation, boldly marching through the perplexity of the internal vessel seemingly unstoppable.

Why?

Pain is a powerful signal, an attention-grabber, a punctuation mark that requires serious circumspection.

With all of its apparent unlimited authority to cause misery, it is invisible, it is illusive.

It cannot be visually documented. But…man has an answer, a cure, grateful relief!

Thousands and thousands of medications with a multiplicity of capabilities:

Pills—all colors and shapes: round, capsules, elliptical, striped, two-toned, taken in different strengths every few hours, twice a day, daily.

Patches—place them anywhere on the body, the medication will find the pain, replace every few days, every week, every month.

Pumps—press only when the offending pain is unbearable.

Reflexology—massage manipulation of muscles by certified therapists with analgesic lotions, oils, and creams.

Herbals—any desired leaf: encapsulated, liquefied, or made frothy.

Sound therapy—music, rhythm, tones, soothing release, or at least, distraction.

Physical therapy—cold compress, warm soak, supportive bandage, passive movement, active exercise.

Apparatus/Equipment—crutches, canes, walkers to relieve pressure and provide support for a designated painful area And when all the "cures" leave the triumphant pain relieving in the fact that it is still aggressively present...

Psychiatry poses the question: "Does this pain really exist?"

When pain this aggressive remains,

The true answer comes not from twenty-first-century science, but Rather from 33 AD phraseology: "By my stripes ye are healed."

Pray!

WHAT DO YOU FEEL?

A babbling brook cascading down to a bubbling pool of crystal clear water…

What do you feel?

The voice of God speaking of the simple beauty of the earth.

Purple mountains towering majestically over blowing emerald fields…

What do you feel?

The magnificent power of God placed beautifully for all to see.

Bumble bees flying effortlessly from plant to plant executing their task, oblivious to all…

What do you feel?

A reminder from God that without those tiny bees, the demise of pollination and the world's food supply would be imminent.

Enormous boulders looming precariously over a dated farmhouse and quiet fields of grain…

What do you feel?

A solemn warning from God that life is tethered by an eyelash and can be instantly destroyed.

Crushed, worn rocks that rest "helplessly" in a driveway or at the edge of quarry…

What do you feel?

The plan of God revealing that every existence can eventually Fade.

While other crushed, worn rocks wait "excitedly" ready to be gathered and placed in crevices to extend life…

What do you feel?

The pain of God revealing that usefulness does continue; it merely changes direction.

Tall, regal redwood trees establish a cool, crisp, protected forest for grateful four-legged inhabitants…

What do you feel?

A blueprint from God that illustrates the unique plan He has implemented on earth so all can exist.

Ocean waves that ebb and flow as time passes each and every day…

What do you feel?

The control of God that maintains the tides that are His and His alone.

The blazing sun seen round the world daily, providing heat, light, and energy needed by all living creatures…

What do you feel?

An assured faith that God has established for us to hold on to, knowing He will provide and will always be there.

REALITY CHECK

YES, GOD IS REAL! A SPIRITUAL CERTAINTY

A SONG OF SOLOMON LOVE STORY

We met as friends of friends and our lives became intertwined.

Both of Godly backgrounds, we were of similar mind.

We read our Bibles together; we attended church and prayed.

We sang and talked of Jesus, but though unplanned we strayed.

Life was good, but something to our Christian backing?

The world was a place that just swallowed us whole,

and made us feel we were knowledgeable and bold.

A new life began; he was darling and sweet,

but that responsibility sent us to a biblical retreat.

Could this possibly be…another on the way?

How could we explain this? What would we say?

Then came to heart, verses from Proverbs 22

so that was the plan; God had broken through!

We had departed, but now we're coming back.

We've asked for God's forgiveness and our God was quick to act.

We were brought up and trained in the way that we should go,

but for the last few years little did it show.

Our God is an awesome God. He put us back on track!

Our family's on the right road now and God said, "Welcome back!"

ALWAYS READY

I don't really know how it started, what came to be routine.

The quiet one-way exchanges left quite time in between.

I had passed her door so many times, ignoring the whispered cells.

One look around the crowded room left my heart in tumbled fall.

In the bed was a demure figure with beautiful hair of gray,

With the warmest eyes I'd ever seen, one could not walk away.

The quiet roar of many machines was disconcerting and depressing.

The weak, small smile she gave to me was indeed my personal blessing.

The whispered calls I ignored so long were, "Baby, baby, baby."

Feeling obligated to talk to her, I learned her name was Sadie.

The conversation was just one way; she didn't know much of her room.

She did seem to know that her prognosis was one of certain doom.

I would stay a while and hold her hand and stroke her beautiful hair.

Of all the visits, regardless of time, there was never anyone there.

I returned many times to relay to her my funny facts of life,

But in all my trips, her lack of guest caused me a lot of strife.

The staff explained, when she arrived, the lawyer was not attentive,

The only thing she wanted was that downturn would be prevented.

I was taught about a special cream to smooth over Sadie's skin,

Being especially careful to avoid places where thin skin had once been.

To sit and watch her recessed, deep in blankets and bedspreads,

Her chest barely rising and falling, left me with a since of dread.

Something kept me coming back, she seemed as a friend would be.

Her body was weak and breathing uncertain, but her mind was sharp and free.

As I would enter, she would say, "Baby, how are things this day?"

And I would answer with all the info of things happening out my way.

"Am I in heaven?" she once asked. "I talk to God each night."

"He told me you were his angel and you would treat me right."

It amazes me some things you do, are not for your own pleasure.

You do the things that God ordains in His time and in His measure.

I brought small things to Sadie; she felt wanted, loved, and content.

And then one day when I returned, Sadie to God had been sent.

Eight months had passed since I first entered, and God had the final word.

Now there's no reason to stop anymore for Sadie's prayer was heard.

I'm really missing Sadie; I learned so much from her smile.

Or maybe it was all God bestowed on me, as I sat with her that while.

His plan is quite specific with varied jobs large and small.

Our job is to be always ready, when by whatever means He calls.

DARKNESS

Our world can be a bright, positive place.
But there also exists dark, negative space.

God has provided all that we need;
He even bestowed in each of our seeds,
individual choices known as free will.
that can negate His plan when choices kill.

The needles, the packets, the spoons, and secret meetings,
leave bodies and souls with their godliness fleeting.

Dependencies, resentment, wrong choices, or depression
have left shrouds of darkness engulfing sound expression.

Fissures take young people and swallow them whole.
The drug and alcohol lure is loud, accessible, and bold.

Bolder than the messages that make addiction clear,
bolder still than any words that initiate and foster fear.
At one time it was the thought; drugs were a social obligation,
but the consequence we now face is a solidly addicted nation.

Even prescribed meds are turning dark and deadly sinister,
for many circumvent doctors to decide when to administer.

The noose is tightening and time is getting short.
This malicious, immoral lifestyle we must firmly now abort.
Go not the path of evil men for the way of the wicked is as darkness.

Cut loose the reins of addiction's hold and use God-given smartness.

God tells us what we should avoid, and He is quite specific,
your whispered word about God's plan could truly be terrific.

All have not heard or may have forgotten that God can take darkness
away.
Trust and hold on, pray for resolve and addicts can see a clean day.

Our world can still be a bright, positive place,
when we receive and understand God-given grace.

EMOTIONS: PLACING A PARENT

Mom required placement to help with her needs.
She was becoming a handful, a stressor indeed.
Her ability to do was becoming less and less,
but making the decision put us all to the test.

To be stuck in a place where there's no up or down,
is one way life makes you feel lassoed and bound.
There is no certainty of which way to go,
but plan for the best so life continues to flow.

Watch what you wish for, for your wish could become prayer.
Search heart and mind completely to inspect the feelings there.
Your brilliant calculations may be focused on need—
but who's to say what's really good or where to put your seed.

For a placement with long-term possibility,
occurred after eight days in a hospital facility.
Physical ability seemed less than it used to be,
mind and thoughts more weakened but definitely free.

The intensity of the months of plotting and intrigue,

resulted in an ending that was difficult to believe.

The wish was granted and the prayer was heard,

but now the mind's "unaccepting" of the long-awaited word.

Mom was whisked one early morn, in emergency status mode,

The ambulance raced through winding streets, with a restricted airway code.

The next eight days were filled with fear, trepidation, and despair.

The future was difficult to fathom then, for what could be looming there.

A haze had settled on the morn, all seemed obscure and cold.

Discussion, yes, multiple times, no settlement yet to behold.

The delicate lady in 306, had caused a care impasse—one wondered how long her ninety-seven years were willing to tenaciously last.

Caregiving was day to day at best; the unexpected was the norm.

So I rose each day and carefully planned to care and do no harm.

It was hard to stand at the foot of her bed, with sad eyes staring at me, waiting for answers that had not come; perhaps prayer was the key.

Where was the faith on which I stood for every hard bump in the road?

Sleepless nights are tear-stained face resulted from carrying the load.

How many times has God said in his Word, "The battle is not yours"?

God again became my resolve and His peace filled all my pores!

GOD WAS IN CONTROL!

Memories From An Adult Son

Dad thought about marriage long before it actually happened.

Finding the right woman took a while.

Then school, jobs, child, rent, his graduation, second child, surprise...

third child and a purchased house.

Hard times at first, struggles, arguments over money, thoughts of divorce, but "something" intervened.

There were arduous places in the road, highs and lows, but the family unit endured.

Looking back over those years of near destruction, now, almost causes a smile.

Praise God Dad knew when times were stressed...

God was in control!

Anything can be a problem if it gets out of hand. It was important to keep everything managed.

It was a challenge to hold the family together and give it all that it needed to flourish.

The house required maintenance; while children required verbalized love and discipline, assistance, active listening, structure, and fun time.

Home life required more than one person to provide it all; so it was God who supplied Dad a help mate that supported and assisted in filling those needs.

Remembering that Mom also needed loving attention and a sincere expression of appreciation at all times, Dad provided both.

Dad knew communication was the key that unlocked troubled moments.

He used the key.

The head of household was responsible for the spiritual realm, morality, and honesty, teaching a positive work ethic and motivation toward success.

He and his help mate were given these monumental tasks.

But, it was necessary for them to remember...

God was in control!

There were pulls in many directions and with Mom (even working), children, house, pets, vehicles, and futures; all required money.

But money was not a volcanic action in this marriage.

Peace and contentment came in faith unseen, but believed.

Between the career, the lawn, the hanging gutter, the oil changes plus the community responsibilities, the homework checking, the dog washing, and the PTA offices...there was the Word!

God was still in control!

Dad had no idea what the future held. He had a plan; he prayed.

He strategized, he discussed it with God, and then he shared it with all of us.

He was the role model that God had placed in our family unit.

There were no promises of success, but success was there and it grew.

Dad's steps were ordered because he knew God was in control!

THANK YOU, JESUS!

Mom sees the little things no one else ever notices.

She tends to know where everything is, even though she did not put it there.

She knows exactly how many dirty clothes are in each hamper, which chore was not done, and who was responsible.

Mom makes the family and the household run like a well-oiled machine.

She's the only one who can work an outside job, stop at the grocery store on her way home, wash and dry two loads of clothes, prepare dinner, check homework, spend some cuddle time, walk the dog, feed the cat, and enjoy prayer time all in the same day.

Thank you, Jesus!

No one answers when dinner choices are requested, but selections are made and food is always served.

No matter which one or two friends drop in, there is always enough to share.

"Take what you have and divide it among the people you have," she always says.

"When it's gone...it's gone."

Who else remembers all the rules of the house, who's on punishment, who said what, and that the meeting is Wednesday and the appointment is Friday?

Thank you, Jesus!

Mom has all the answers:

Catch the dryer when it buzzes and you won't have to iron.

It's okay to take the last one and throw the box away.

If it's not in the hamper, it won't be washed.

If you don't fold and return, your drawers will be empty.

Everything has a place and should be returned there when not in use.

Trash cans are emptied daily.

And she knows when to say, "Ask your father."

Thank you, Jesus!

Who is it that never gets to go to bed early or sleep late?

Who cannot afford to be sick?

Who goes nonstop without complaining?

Who prays continuously for her family unit and for the head of her household?

Thank you, Jesus…for Mom!

OF EXCESS

I really like the way it looks, I think I like the sway.
My closet calls to buy this one, to save for a rainy day.
I'd better leave it in the trunk, until it becomes somewhat "old."
"You don't need another social dress," are words I would be told.

I'll hang it in the upstairs room; no, I think that one is packed.
Better put it in the room downstairs, and slip it in the back.
I was really lucky to find that sale; it was truly a wonderful catch.
Tomorrow I'll go see if I can find bag and shoes to match.

Think of those around the world, who have no room of clothes;
in fact, the few things that are owned stay under pillows in folds.
There are no choices of what to wear; if worn today for it's hot,
will be donned tomorrow to be worn again, even if it's not.

We have clothes for color and seasons, for events and purpose too.
We have such mass collections; they take lengthy time to view.
And then there are the scarves and bags, hats, and shoes galore.
It should be years before any of us steps in another store.

Why do we buy to such excess, in a year how many are worn?

Do we really go to that many events, so all can be adorned?

Are we patting ourselves on the back to show we have arrived?

Or have we set goals that we must reach and thus we continue to strive.

What could we do instead of shop…how about volunteer?

Our children need lots of additional aid to help their ships to steer.

There is the fact that we are buying, could the money be better spent?

So many charities are in dire need, so donate and help make a dent.

Many help groups need gently used clothes that would be meaningful to obtain.

Giving needy persons down on their luck, support with self-worth to regain.

Jesus tells us to heal, cleanse, and give; that thought should refresh and give hope.

As we share from our storehouse and aid those in need, we're helping individuals cope.

INSTANTANEOUS

Waiting for a dial tone...waiting for a traffic light...waiting for an elevator...

We don't wait well!

Waiting for water to boil...waiting for someone to finish a sentence...waiting for a friend...

We don't wait well!

Waiting for grills to get hot...waiting to be served...waiting for the line to move...

Two minutes—too long... *WE DON'T WAIT WELL!*

Where did this evil come from? Impatience has reared an ugly head and the results are astounding: frustration...cell phones...finger tapping...iPods...anger...vocal lashes...rapidly changing technology...road rage...finishing sentences for others...the Internet...all adding more fuel to the fire...literally!

We want what we want and we want it, NOW! All that we wait for will happen, but not quickly enough for our time frame.

Why are we so intolerant?

Plates are full. Blackberries are jammed with information: schedules, e-mails addresses, and texting abilities. Instantaneous contact!

Texting slow?—go to e-mail. Email too slow?—head to Twitter.

After a second of thought, maybe the information wasn't worth sending after all.

Even newspapers have fallen victim to impatience. Newspapers are being dismantled because there are now super fast media accesses to news. No one has to wait for the morning paper. Updates?

Head to the Internet or 24/7 news stations.

How did life get to be this way?

We tend to rely too much on technology—the faster the better. We schedule appointments and meetings without considering prep time, travel time, or time of day. We overbook. We wait until the last minute. And then we want "haste" to immediately make the scheduling work for us. Our plan is wrong.

Where are we going with these instantaneous demands? Is instant gratification the next fundamental rule? "Satisfied are they that yell and scream the loudest, throw fits of anger the most, or destroy the human spirit with vile words."

Time is appointed by God. We cannot fix it, rush it, change it, or save it. Time is not instantaneous. It occurs in regimented order…God's order. The Word does not instruct to hurry, rush, speed, or hasten in positive. It does say to hasten with your feet is sinning (Proverbs 19:2).

We do not have to be slow and lingering. We need to be deliberate, but aware of time. Include all possible deterrents in the preplanning stages, anything that might detain you from meeting your on-time goal. When you feel the need to become instantaneous, breathe deeply. Count 1…2…3…4…10…The time to breathe and count may be the time it takes NOT to exhibit rude, distasteful behavior. God wants us to cease from anger and delight in peace. Patience is executed with calmness. Plan well, wait patiently, and your desires shall be expectedly attained.

LONG-STANDING FRIENDSHIPS

The days don't matter; the memories are strong.
The time spent together is a treasure.
Hugs and laughter, chatter on and on;
the emotions is beyond gauge or measure.

Maybe you met at a school long ago.
And have kept in touch since then.
Or perhaps a co-worker's tight connection
grew to become your best friend.

The heart understands and the talk is easy;
it has been years since we last met.
But time slips by as the warmth does engulf;
reconnection is a confident bet.

Spouses, children, activities, and style
are all fair game as you share.
Past information has been sorted and stored
so continuance of the saga is there.

The miles may be distant but don't matter at all.

Once connected, the stirring is real.
The meeting time permits a burst of emotion
that allows the release your heart feels.

It's amazing how much info needs to be exchanged,
every joy, every heartache, every pain,
is shared from both sides of the buddy fence
with self-confidence and assurance to gain.

Long-standing friendships bring inner relief;
the time frame is of no account.
Whenever the "let's meet" possibilities arise
jump quickly and plan grand amounts.

PERSONAL TRAUMA

July, 1954—Hit by a car in segregated Alabama, injuries ignored by officials

April 10, 1963—Father died suddenly

August 17, 1966—Left for college 250 miles away, alone

May 8, 1970—"F" on transcript in swimming, can't graduate? First to graduate without required swimming

June 30, 1973—Married, moved to NC the next day

March 25, 1974—Son born after near-death delivery

December 19, 1981—Moved to new house with stairs, first diagnosis, severe arthritis

April 14-16, 1988—Mother-in-law moved to NC, my first knee surgery

August 19, 1992—Son taken to college in VA, empty-nest

July 24, 1994—Mother and her husband moved to NC

January 28, 1995—Mom's husband placed in facility, congested heart failure and lost a leg

November 1, 1995—My husband out-placed, no job

February 16, 1996—Cancer? Not cancer? My second surgery, breast biopsy

December 17, 1997—Total shoulder reconstruction, third surgery

October 13, 1998—First right knee replacement, fourth surgery

November 8, 1998—Husband critically injured in work-related accident ten days after I was discharged from the hospital

June 30, 1999—Retirement, arthritis, and knee took me out of the classroom

September and December, 1999—Uncle and Mom's husband died unexpectedly

April 14, 2000—Told I am diabetic

January 22, 2001—Mom had a serious stroke

April 1, 2001—Left my home and moved in with Mom

April 30, 2002—My husband and I, Mom, and Mother-in-law purchased and moved into a handicapped-ready house

March 4, 2005—Second right knee replacement surgery, Mom had a second stroke eight days earlier

August 11, 2006—Brother in coma in Baltimore, first of many trips

August 22, 2006—Mother-in-law suffered a major, paralyzing stroke

May 19, 2008—Took Mom to see her son, my brother, in Baltimore; I suffered a severe fall from the van.

June 28, 2008—Brother died

July 3, 2008—Planned funeral, traveled, gave the eulogy at my brother's funeral

September 8, 2008—Third right knee replacement surgery, discovered leg was broken in the May fall

January 4, 2009—Stress fracture in right leg

April 22, 2009—Torn left rotator cuff, probably happened in the May 2008 fall

January 26, 2010—Eye exam, told blindness would probably occur within the year, surgery both eyes, God fixed it! Sight secure!

December 6, 2010—Driving home, car in ditch, out of ditch, over a driveway, hit a brick column, into a fence post, splintered a cable box, destroyed several saplings, slammed into an oak tree… injured, but "walked" away

Some dates will truly live in one's memory for a lifetime. Trauma is not always the result of bad things. The preceding dates might seem massive number. However in the 23,546 days that I have lived,

only about thirty-nine provided me with serious traumatic experiences. Praise God! Life is good.

Substitute your personal dates that you will probably have no difficulty recalling.

It may be asked, "How can one remember the exact dates?"

Those traumatic moments hold such heartache or disappointment,

shock, or pain, even exhilaration or joy, that the dates are buried into your heart, your mind, and your spirit forever.

The occurrences are life changing.

The old adage says: "Time heals all wounds [and traumas.]" But the adage does not say how much time is needed for the healing or resolve to take place. It does not tell you what to do and it does not provide a "How to Recover Guide."

So what do you do during the wait time?

- Remember cherished times and the God-given abilities you possess. They far outnumber the traumas.
- Pray that God will ease the hurt and help you to live through it. There is an exit.
- Have a support system to lean on, include our Heavenly Father first.

- Take care of yourself sensibly; follow a routine, rest, eat healthy, and include moments you enjoy in your day.

- Don't fall off the deep end. Stay in the Word. Include time for quiet meditation.

- Look forward without those pull-down phrases filling your mind, "I wish I had…" or "If only I hadn't…" or "I should have seen…" or "It was my fault…"

- Stay positive.

Dear Father, I give you all praise, honor, and glory. You are omnipotent. You know what has happened in my life. The unexpected is so hard to understand and accept. The hurt and restrictions that have been caused in my life are debilitating, but I know your plan for my life has highs and lows, joy and pain. I place my situation in your hands as I stand on your Word and rest in your arms. In every dark cloud there is a silver lining that must be found and internalized. Order my steps to follow the path that will lead me out of any trauma and back to a productive life lived for the up building of your kingdom. In the mighty name of Jesus, who can right my ship, I pray. Amen.

BLACK HISTORY: LOOK BACK TO APPRECIATE AND LEARN... LOOK FORWARD TO PLAN SUCCESS!

"Stormy" The Road We've Trod

As I look around, I am surrounded by living history! History from the fields of North Carolina, the coal mines of Pennsylvania and labor in other states, from the factories, from the kitchens and bathrooms of whites, from normal schools, colleges, schoolhouses, classrooms, pulpits, businesses, lunch counters, buses, and offices. There can be found inspiration and aspiration. As a people, we look back and lament our stormy road, express grief at the wrongs that we have been subjected to, and are remorseful at the length of time it has taken to get to this point. But…we cannot stand with our backs to the future as we reminisce.

We have learned much from our past history. We learned that we had the physical strength to endure the middle passage journey from the Motherland to America and to survive the harsh exposure and treatment on the plantations of the South. We learned how to survive the attack dogs and the full force of the fire hoses during the Civil Rights Movement. We have learned that racism is now subliminal, but still here, so the battle continues. *We learned that we are a strong people!*

Early on we escaped, moved north, attached ourselves to people who could and would help us. While we mourned the loss of loved ones at the hands of the "master," we created a new way of life for ourselves. We had determination during the initial flight north, as we later marched, sat, and were jailed to make gains that should have already been ours. *We are a determined people!*

Our existence has been firmly and spiritually connected to God our Father. We sang spirituals as praise, ("Amen," "I'm on the Battlefield," "I'm Gonna Sing"); we sang for motivation, ("Great Day!" "Walk with Me," "Ole Time Religion"); we sang to communicate ("Wade in the Water," which might have meant "meet at the river tonight"; "Over My Head," which could have been a signal that the overseer was watching from his tower; or "Steal Away," that could have meant the time to escape was imminent). As people we tend to sing, praise, and worship with much emotion and feeling. We have learned to stay God-connected. *We are a spiritual people!*

Over the decades, fathers have gone away to earn a better living for their families. Men, who did not return, left children and children's children for wives and mothers to rear. Today, many of our households are still headed by females; and yet we continue to survive and move forward. Regardless of the amount of earnings, there is food. Regardless of education, there is honest work.

Regardless of how many reside in a house, there is shelter. God has provided! *We are a praying people!*

In 1868, a constitutional amendment was legally adopted that guaranteed equal protection under the law for all people. Today, what can definitely be said is, "They are still working on it."

In 1968, a hundred years later, the reigning thought was that the United States was moving toward two societies—one black and one White, separate and unequal.

In 2009, forty-one years after that pronouncement, there was a black man who was elected to the highest political office in the land.

That's new! But the bigger news is that he was supported and elected by blacks, Hispanics, and whites! Are we now on a less stormy road?

Or are the subliminal prejudices still actively present in our behavioral patterns and individual interactions of today?

We had our share of lightning and thunder, rain and wind, and *still* we have survived to see another day. Survival has allowed us to put our ideas into action, our interventions into production, our thoughts into books, and our children in high places! We hold prestigious offices and sit on prominent boards. We own businesses in wide-ranging fields. We occupy positions in every profession, but those advances are not enough. We should not have to fight until blood flows for every bit of forward progress we attain. For what God has provided for us, we know… *We are a blessed people!*

So, as we remember the wars and the depressions lived through, the lean times, the contributions we've made, and the background experience we've gained, we praise God that we are here and are able to boldly prepare for a future that offers the potential for success! We must plan for that success by working harder, praying, listening, getting involved, voting, writing letters, or by being a mentor or role model to a young person. If we donate, be it time or money, donate to an organization or cause where people in need are the recipients of our actions. *We have the capacity of success in our hands. Hold tight! Don't let it slip away!*

TRAVEL WITH THE ELDERLY... GOD IS SO GOOD!

In the air…On the rail…On the road…
God Is So Good!

Limitation…Hesitation…Special reservation…
God Is So Good!

Strangers help…Conductors assist…Schedules fit…
God Is So Good!

Much luggage accommodated…Movement possible…Cooperation
abundant…
God Is So Good!

Unexpected happens…A moment to recoup…No time for tears…
God Is So Good!

Matters not what transpires…Matters not where you are…
Matters only that it is understood…
Our God Is Oh So Good!

WHO IS THY NEIGHBOR?

Inspired By Luke 10:25-37

Open Spaces: Sidewalks

Squares with joints methodically planned,

Hard surfaces, random cracks,

Faces coming and going, all different, yet the same.

All hiding hurts, wounds or despair.

We pass the faces of unknowns daily.

So, who *is* thy neighbor? What can we give?

Closed Spaces: Malls

Shiny, automatic glass, rows and rows of rectangular spaces filled with cars.

Brand-name bags, boxes, and totes brush by.

A soul sits silently by one door, modest clothes, empty hands, downward glance.

The recipient of judgmental glances; he still does not move.

Who *is* thy neighbor? What can we give?

Required Spaces: Job Sites

Patterned cubicles, monitors, keyboards, family pictures, in-out files,

Surrounded by various levels of updated technology.

Each geometric unit is occupied by an individual.

One who has hopes, dreams, and aspirations…but who also experiences overload,

Confusion and depression.

Still, who *is* thy neighbor? What can we give?

Anytime, anywhere, all who you meet are neighbors. We can:

Extend a hand, get involved, greet with a smile, feel something within, communicate, give of ourselves and give from our abundance.

Listen to and be aware of all the "neighbors" in your village.

WHY MY CHILD?

How deep is the cut, with the loss of a child,

For from God he is ours for just a little while.

We smile as we think back to a long ago time,

And recall those brief words, "Boy, that son of mine!"

The thoughts of hearty laughter slowly drifting by,

It makes me stop and wonder, "O dear God, why?"

The lengthy conversations during many times of strife

Brought close family feelings as we struggled with life.

Choices and decisions, highs and lows to face,

Preparation for the impending and for running life's race.

You blessed me, kind Father, with manna from the sky,

But sitting here so quietly, I can't help but wonder, "Why?"

I've lived in the Word and I know he's not here,

His soul is now free; he has nothing to fear.

No pain, no heartache, no worry…just peace,

He believed in you, Master, and has gained his release.

He's happily rejoicing, with family again met,

All existing in a place without grief, toil, or sweat.

My son has transcended, what lessons can be learned?

Live each day as your last and a reward will be earned.

With much love I thank you for loaning me your child,

My peace is he's resting with you for awhile.

So, I guess as I ponder, in my heart I do know why,

Successful completion here means a mansion on high!

WINGLESS ANGELS

The doorbell rang, who could that be?
I raised the door to see males one, two, three.
Big smiles did greet me, with a suspicious looking glint,
a very quick inquiry asking, "Why were they sent?"
A surprise was the answer that caused me a flutter;
they smiled and they chuckled and looked at each other.
"A dishwasher we've brought for we heard there was need,
if it's okay with you we would like to proceed."
My heart was pounding with deafening precision,
I cannot refuse, was my split-second decision
Our dishwasher had died way back in July,
so how did they know why did they buy?
A casual comment had been made between friends
that brought us to this day, to this shocking end.
Our Awesome God sent this grand surprise;
a lump in my throat was beginning to rise.
"Sit down and relax and read of your new toy.
We're happy to do this to bring you some joy."
Only God knows how deeply I was touched;
the feelings inside were almost too much.
Thank you, Wingless Angels for your spirit of giving love.

and we know in our hearts, this is a gift from above.
We praise God to the highest for allowing us to know
friends with His spirit who are not afraid to show
the love of His kingdom through whatever they do,
with humble sincerity we thank the three of you.
(And all those faceless angels who stand behind you—
God always sends what you need.)

ALLOW ME TO INTRODUCE…

PEOPLE IN CIRCUMSTANCES!
MORE ALIKE THAN DIFFERENT

BABY BUNDLE

God's little miracle, so soft the touch,
he possesses parts of people that his parents love so much.
Eyes from Nana, nose like Mom is found,
long slender fingers to Granddad's tightly bound.
Head shape like Daddy, pursed lips that seem to show,
that this special boy child elicits quite a glow.
With all the possibilities and roads he can embrace,
The world is his orchard, with fullness and with grace.
A child is an investment; many deposits must be made,
to insure a successful ending, a plan should be carefully laid.
Moral understanding, respect, ethics, and love
along with motivation and the Word sent from above.
The job of rearing children is a massive one at best,
with Murphy's Law established, the challenge is a test.
Call on those with knowledge, the elders have nearly all,
but friends and books are gainful for answers when you call.
The world's a scary shrinking place, with evil high and low;
be sure your child is Lord enriched, and he'll know how to grow.

BLACK FEMALE

The lips are large, the bust full, and the ample hips create a strong foundation.

She emerges as tall, short, and all heights in between, in shades from the deepest ebony to the creamiest sand.

Short, black, crinkled hair; long, silky, brown hair…a mixture of generations long past.

Flourishing with strong determination, she places her finger on the pulse of life around her.

She is willing to give and share with others or she is capable of going it alone, if circumstances command it be so.

Life has played cruel tricks on God's supposedly weaker sex of color.

She has stood on slave blocks and has lain in masters' beds.

She was the last to receive education, usually during stolen moments.

Her marriages seemed destined to be short lived, for men were jailed, drugged, or untamed.

Jobs that were menial, dead-end, or provided unfair compensation were left for her.

Loaded with responsibility, from absent husbands or irresponsible children, this female's cadence went from child, to mistress to mother, perchance wife, to grandmother, then returning to mother as black women worldwide raise cherished grandchildren as their own.

As chapter after chapter of this life unfolds, the statement might be made:

"What a dismal existence!"

But that statement would be far from the truth.

For this woman, this black female knows from where her strength comes.

She understands and utilizes the power of prayer.

She is persistent, passionate, and dedicated to whatever purpose she champions.

The ability to speak to convince...work to stabilize...comfort to heal...or love to build up is hers.

She can perfectly boast of an education of preponderance and position; intelligence that has catapulted her into board rooms, executive offices, and elected office.

What sustains and motivates her is her love of God and the protection of her vessel for His habitation.

This is a female who can be an intense wife supporting her husband, while maintaining the responsibility of rearing and nurturing children, and still be a strong, professional woman.

She can provide for her family by working hours each day outside the home, returning to labor additional hours at home, in the most creative ways.

She claims whatever is needed to make ends meet and make life work for her family.

The black female has been victorious and will continue to be.

Her praises to God, her study of the Word to gain God's power, her use of God-given talents, and her prayers of intercession, will assure her lasting success!

Though life's road is never ribbon smooth or laser precise, it is certain that when situations become challenging, this female remains focused and resilient.

For her endurance, she has triumphed as a survivor!

CAREGIVERS

Middle of the day, middle of the night, caregivers get the call.

Come assist, help, fetch, or feed, caregivers handle it all.

The heartstrings pull; one views the sight of parents who were once strong and bold.

Now time has taken a wicked swing, and Mom or Dad seem quite old.

Both gave so much to children and life, for the years and years they lived.

Now it seems that after tying a shoe, they have no more energy to give.

The movements are slow, more deliberate now; days long, time has slowed.

The eyes a little dimmer, the skin a little thinner, and bones are now fragile and bowed.

These golden years may not be polished, as years of planning hoped they'd be…

God has provided a thoughtful, loving child who gives and gives for free.

A no-charge endeavor is given to parents and it fits like a devoted glove.

The long hours they spend, are caring and kind, and pay a distinct type of love.

For caregivers are very special folk, who step in and fill the gap, Tasks above their daily routine, so a pool of reserve strength is tapped.

For Mom and Dad have paid their dues, and now as shadows fall…

A grateful child steps up to the plate, to manage and carry the ball.

Are parents in need appreciative? Of course, for this is their child.

In case there is doubt, stand quietly by and watch lips curl to a smile.

SUPPORT OF A FRIEND

First seven days…spirit destroyed…last seven, on top of the world!

Two weeks later, back to the center Cancer Center for another scheduled session.

Pumped! Ready to go! Hurry up!

Blood pressure…great! Blood levels…fantastic! It's a go!

Hurry up!

Numbed with Lidocaine an hour before! Ready!

Attached the port…Praise God, no pain, it hit the back! Yea!

Hurry up!

Saline in…Push! Push! Okay, draw back the blood.

What! No blood! Raise arm…turn head…cough…lift chin… stand up…bend…stretch…nothing!

No blood!

Loosen clothing…recline…raise your legs…lie back fully extended…

No blood!

Extract and reconnect…manipulate…press…squeeze…

Nothing! A piercing, silent scream heard with the eyes!

That pumped high at arrival…? Gone!

Dizziness comes…floating spots come…pounding headache comes.

Everything stops! Frustration…irritation…progress hindered…

Today was supposed to go so smoothly. The best laid plans…

Why won't it work? Why won't the blood flow out?

"Please God, please! Let the blood flow forth."

"Why this dreadful headache? That's new."

Pharmacy order! Medication! Rest thirty minutes! Wait!

Lidocaine the culprit…Too much of it! Rest…wait!

Try again. Please God…blood! Think butterflies! Be calm!

Eight thousand four hundred seconds before success. The link is running in both directions!

Saline in…blood out! Praise God!

The process continues. Bag hung…injections made…next bag hung…pain gone…smiles…chatter…patience…prayer!

Cancer kills…but with God and support, cancer can be killed.

Chemo Treatment #3

LOVE THEM

The seniors in our lives are precious gems.
We extend love and care for them.

They've paid their dues and now can rest,
though long life and health can be a test.

Think of the years they gave their all,
and always rose to answer their call.

They sacrificed and cried, but made life flow;
we are grateful for the seeds seniors did sow.

And now as it's nearer to their heavenly rest,
they deserve that we give them our loving best.

So take a deep breath and give them a hug,
and give them the best of our undying love.

MEMORIES OF LAWRENCE

Since I have known Lawrence longer than most, I thought it would be appropriate to provide some insight into my introverted brother, whom I loved dearly. I begin with the words: loving, playful, and caring, even talkative, because that was our childhood. I can remember sitting at the foot of each others' bed as children, especially when we were sick, talking for hours. I remember fighting over who would get nickels, dimes, and quarters from the green recliner.

That was Daddy's favorite chair and when he reclined to watch TV, his pockets would empty into the chair. There were always enough coins found there for ice cream or banana split candies—Lawrence's favorites.

We both loved scary movie that came on late night television. At that time, the only television in the house was on the first floor in the den next to the kitchen. None was in any of the bedrooms on the second floor. On Friday and Saturday nights, we would watch horror movies on that television and after being frightened to death for several hours, would race through the house to get upstairs to the safety of our bedrooms, so the "monsters" wouldn't get us. Many times the lights were left on downstairs because neither of us slowed down long enough to turn them off.

I remember mischievous times—swinging on one of the lower kitchen cabinet doors as children would do; the door broke off its hinges. Lawrence was the one with a "clever" idea for repair—use Vaseline to hold the door in place and no one would notice it was broken. Seemed like a good idea at the time and it worked for a while, until the door began to slowly slide downward. We chose not to explain how the Vaseline got on the cabinet door frame in the first place, which made matters worse. And of course, we endured the punishment together. We did everything together.

Lawrence enjoyed a normal childhood, going to church from a young age, singing in the choir, participating in YPD (Young People's Department), going on church outings, and palling around with friends we shared. Lawrence loved riding his bike, playing pool, watching television, and was quite skilled at playing the piano. He really enjoyed listening to cassette tapes and to the radio. He also loved bowling, chess, and other activities. In spite of all of these distractions, Lawrence was actually a good student and like school a lot.

Then at age thirteen for him and seventeen for me, our father died and Lawrence became a different person. Still loving and caring, but now introverted and quiet. Mom and I never really knew what he was thinking. He ran away once as a teen and stayed away three days. He went eight blocks to our aunt's house and called home after a few hours to report his location.

Shortly after I left for college, even though 1966 was early for computer availability, he enrolled in the Philadelphia Computer Institute. We had no computer at home but he spent early mornings And late afternoons there to complete assignments. Upon graduating with honors, he enlisted in the U.S. Air Force to work with computer technology and programming. There he continued to use that expertise for the next eighteen plus years. Afterwards, he worked at NSA near Laurel, Maryland, still with computers and still indirectly for the government. His last job was with Computer Sciences Corporation, where he continued to work with his beloved computers. Nothing frightened Lawrence more than the fact that his computers might lack the newest upgrades available. He stayed on top of the all advances in technology.

Lawrence had a very dry wit that showed itself at the oddest times. While visiting the Frankford Rehabilitation Facility where he spent his last two years, he dramatically threw his sheet and gown to the floor. The nurse told him if he was going to strip, he should at least charge for viewing. She suggested $2.00, then said, "You're a handsome young man, better make it $4.00." Lawrence looked at her, smiled, and said, "$6.00." I told him he couldn't collect, because he didn't have a G-string to put the money under.

He looked at me…same smile, and said, "Slide it under my feeding tube." He had his share of highs and lows, struggles and triumphs, but he always seemed to come out on the "bright side."

Lawrence's hobbies included: photography pursuits, all areas of technology, and making sure his computers did not become antiquated. He loved to cook and from a young teen he thrived on reproducing recipes he had obtained from television. He did not travel much in later years and my family missed having him visit during summer. The only way for Mom to see him was to head north and she had the opportunity to do that one last time. Mom, at ninety-six, did not travel either. But she was truly blessed because she had that chance to visit Lawrence on two of his "good days," which were few…six weeks later he died. I am so grateful for taking the trip because that visit was a blessing shared.

Our country really owes a debt of gratitude to Lawrence Franklin Saunders. He worked with a sense of duty, with talent and dedication. The Air Force entrusted him with responsibility and he executed and respected it. Lawrence loved the USA, whether it was being thrown out of the bed by an earthquake while stationed in Japan or crawling through the jungles of Panama, he loved doing his part to make the United States a great, safe, place to live.

One of the really good things that came from Lawrence being in the Air Force, was that while stationed in Thailand, he met and later married Ko Kyong Cha, (a.k.a. Casey) and they had one son, Daniel. Casey and Daniel were the very best things that could have happened to my brother. Our family thanks God for her loving Lawrence for their thirty-five years, especially these last few difficult ones. Lawrence's wife and son have put thousands of miles on odometers, and hundreds of dollars in toll baskets going back and forth between Laurel and Baltimore to visit at the facility. There they would sit with him when he was comatose, cut his hair, cut his nails, rub his peeling skin, talk to him even when he was not coherent, feed him (when he was eating), fuss at him when he needed it, and just love him. Daniel was a God-sent angel and his dad would still be very proud of his twenty-seven years.

In 2003, I wrote a book of verse and thoughts, *On Any Given Day…A Butterfly May Cross Your Path*, and I included memories of my brother in it. I bring closure here with an excerpt from, *Somehow… Seems Long Ago:*

(VERSE 1)

Inseparable as young siblings—

A girl/a boy, sister/brother, friends

Same travel buddies, same interests, same hangouts.

Sat on the front porch together, Sat on the top concrete step of the row house, side by side—

together, Sat at the foot of each other's bed…talking…strangely enough to each other.

Engaged in mischief together and endured the punishment together.

Three and a half years between birth dates, but mutual encouragement, respect, and love.

Lots of actions occurred that brought us to…now. (2003)

(VERSE 6)

Letters—none, calls—none, visits—none.

What happens to a relationships that was nurtured, attended to, and supported?

Where did the caring, the concern, the laughter go?

Was it lost among other actions, travel, or growing up?

Can the giving and sharing, hoping and trusting be regained?

Can that warmth for, interest in, and love toward one another be rekindled?

Well now, I can answer those questions. Over these last few years, Lawrence and I reconnected and recaptured a lost relationship, a lost friendship. God sometimes puts you in the strangest places; not together in the hometown that we both loved, not in the place that I have lived for thirty-six years, not in his adopted hometown of Laurel, Maryland…but in a rehab facility in Baltimore. I thank God for the opportunity to have again touched each other's heart.

There are many things that I did not get to say to Lawrence and there are many stories that Lawrence took home to God. But when we were given a chance to reconnect, we grabbed it. Don't let any opportunity to reclaim a lost relationship pass you by. Death may interrupt planned good intentions. Remember, death *is* promised, and can abort the best laid plans because its designated time and place are undetermined.

PARADIGM OF CARING

Sincere inquiry, holding hands with both eyes, understanding phrases,

    comfortable enough on both sides to share,

white coat, blue scrubs, lots of years of intense study to gain not only

    knowledge and know-how, but time to "learn" people.

It takes an exceptional medical personality to be able to:

Established confidence

    Listen actively

        Allow for exchange

            Spend necessary time

                Diagnose accurately

                    Gather information in varying ways

                        Use technology and testing wisely

                        Be a friend

Over a span of fifteen to thirty years, the time needed to arrive at this point has been granted, but not all physicians attain such status.

Medical practices are really the people, the doctors, and the staff.

They must pull from a storage tower of behaviors and procedures that fit a multiplicity of problems and personalities.

Few do it right.

To those who have "done it right," salutations and blessings from one who feels especially fortunate to have been directed to "the best."

The best…those doctors who know God and who know they are not He.

Our medical providers also need encouragement. Give it.

Patients need to accept responsibility for personal health. Take it.

God will bless both sides of the equation!

PRAYER FOR MY SISTER

I pray for you, my sister, for you are the chosen one.

You do the work of many; there is so much to be done.

The words that you've been given are housed inside your soul.

They calm, enlighten, proclaim, and teach; their virtue is pure gold.

A teen may need to hear your tone, because of traumatic life.

Select with care, for your rendition can save from wicked strife.

A senior needs a seasoned style, to recall how things were done;

one with patience, love, and care or resignation will have won.

Couples need a special word, to seal worn jagged edges.

So rushing, working, hurting, or fatigue won't plunge in stony wedges.

Leader of worship, speaker of the hour, teacher for a VBS week,

place awesome responsibility, and it's God's face she must seek.

Meditation, contemplation, quiet moments, prayer—

study these major components and God will meet you there.

For presenting to the spiritual side is a monumental task;

preparation for imparting the Word requires planning to make it last.

I pray for you, my sister, that with each word you instill,

presents the path that all should take, understand God's plan and will.

SENIORS, STILL CONTRIBUTING

Keep moving forward!

You never reach the age when you can sit down and do nothing.

Listen, attend discussion groups, vote knowledgeably, write letters, tutor, or mentor.

Share your life stories with others, especially young people.

Correct misbehavior when it is "safe" to do so.

Sometimes young people don't understand respecting elders.

Share your collection of recipes while memories are solid.

How can we continue making Granny's fantastic pound cake or lemon squares, if she never shares the secret ingredients?

Be involved with those who may be different from you. (age, color, culture, or religion)

Pray for all races, for we are far more alike than we are different.

Always be the role model, for you never know who's watching.

Your past years of experience are what will provide wisdom for our future.

TREE PEOPLE

I hope it was a dream last night,
of a tree in the forest—a hideous sight.
The trunk was dark with huge nodules outcast;
it looked rather ominous with an ill-fated past.
I tried to circumvent this strange, mysterious tree,
when much to my surprise, it spoke out to me.
"It's unusual for anyone to walk all this way,
but Lord knows I needed someone this day.
As you can tell, I'm different from the others;
I've asked many times to make me like my brothers.
I am tall and stately, and provide breezes blown,
I make available spaces to house nature's own.
Because my trunk is thick, I can't bend in the wind.
But to the forest floor my leaves do I send.
I am unusually large so much shade can I provide,
a place for a picnic, or for children to hide.
I am very strong with the ability to speak
and that little fact makes me vulnerable and weak."
He told me he was an outcast because he could talk,
but sadly God did not give him the ability to walk.
"For I would leave this place for a kinder situation,

a place to be accepted without discrimination.

That place does not exist for any of God's kind.

For others make assumptions with their tiny little minds.

Instead of accepting individuals as they appear to be,

the tendency is to reject, because they're not like me."

God sent me deep into the forest for a reason unknown to me,

to have this strange discussion with a beautifully unique tree.

I told my newfound friend, he was one of a kind and rare,

and what his brothers thought of him, he really should not care.

I rubbed his bark, said my good-byes, no longer could I stay,

but thanked the Lord for our exchange and what I'd learned that day.

Initial impressions can be tainted by assumptions that are wrong.

Accepting information makes positive connections strong.

So walk the path with open heart and mind astute, carefree,

with luck and guidance you may find new knowledge from a tree.

WE ARE BLESSED!

We are grateful for the life that God took to her reward.

She gave much and took great care to follow her dear Lord.

God made mothers special so they know just what we need,

someone to nurture and protect the young lives of God's seed.

Someone to teach from the very start, how difficult life can be,

also to share survival knowledge and how to be set free.

From diapers to toodlers to preschool and more,

she provided the learning that we needed to store.

Mom knew what we required to avoid any dubious lure.

She listened to our problems, to teach what to ignore.

The trauma of our teenage years caused her hair to turn seriously gray.

The clothes, the curfews, activities, and friends were major, back in the day.

We made it through and adulthood arrived, but the upheaval didn't stop there.

On scene she was with advice to give that was timely and perfectly fair.

We lived our lives and moved away, but kept Mom very close.

She was the one, as God had planned, that we would lean on most.

We are grateful for all our family, but somehow the ties did bind
and made our cherished mother, in some ways totally "mine."

Thank you, Father, for providing a mother,
who was truly herself…unlike any other.

WOMAN OF FAITH

I am a woman!

I cannot be crushed, for I stand on the promises of God.

I will not be diminished, for I believed what God has said.

I find no amusement in being brushed aside, for I am God's child.

I am bold and I stand tall, for I am a Woman of Faith!

When my day is jammed with demands from every side and all my best efforts are dashed to the ground…

I retreat to the Word, for it soothes my spirit with the knowledge that for all things there is a time, and that works done in truth, by His children, shall stand.

When the offspring of God's child is lured by the world to the depths of hell, because he or she has forgotten the religious upbringing, on which he teethed, crawled, and walked…

I reclaim my clarity with the Word, remembering that a child trained in the way he should go, will not depart from it.

When my finances shatter and there are seemingly no avenues of resolution to move my budget to stability…

I baptize my mind with God's message from the Word that my supplications will be heard and that all my needs will be supplied.

I rest on His promises and I am at peace, because I am a Woman of Faith and my faith will keep me strong.

Life itself is orchestrated by God as a brief moment in time.

A challenge to all, but especially for a woman, for I above all want the best for my family and the best for myself!

God has given me my road map for life and that map reveals His plan.

No matter how rushed or burdened, how fatigued, depressed, or overwhelmed I become…

It is God's promises in His Word and His revelations in my life that I know

As a Woman of Faith…I am blessed!

YOUNG BLACK MALE

Set jaw, strong calves, imposing chest, with piercing eyes…the signature characteristics of the black male.

His past seems lurid and dark from being stolen, beaten, and having his freedoms restricted.

Nations have been built on his back, for slave labor was available and cheap.

His sweat and blood have been left in the sands of time…across several continents.

Some have succumbed to indecision, bad decisions, or are wandering aimlessly, laboring under no decision at all about the future.

Others have maintained the bitter taste of hatred and disparity, unfairness, and prejudice that have haunted black men for centuries.

Few have shaken the shackles of doom to grab the brass ring from life's carousel. A ring that could possibly balance his blackness, that is so important because of the testimony of the past, with his talent.

When? How? Who?

When will the sun rise on the prospect and possibility of what the future could hold?

How can the hurt, the harm, and the damage that is set so deeply into his soul, be, if not eradicated…soothed?

Who is strong enough, wise enough, or caring enough to pull this task together?

The answer must come from within the circle of this young male's existence.

The only way to defeat the negativism and the prejudice of the past and brighten the look into the future is with an unassailable education, a strong support system, internal motivation and determination, along with an unshakeable faith in God and in himself.

From whence does all this come?

What empties the prison of those falsely accused only because of their color or those at the end of their possibilities?

How can the chains be broken and the breakthrough be found?

If it takes a village to raise a child, especially a black male child, make sure God is in the village.

CELEBRATE!

The Joy Of Living!
Every Day Is A Blessing!

ACCOLADES!

Worship: raise your hands, shout a word, clap, resonate a sound,
Twirl a feeling, sway emotion, praises should never be bound.

Eyes bright; eyes wide; teary, pensive eyes,
Open hearts, receiving minds, make resolutions wise.

Stand from your seat, bow heads in meditation,
Hallelujah to the Father makes for earnest dedication.

Giving from the heart or offering a helping hand,
Sharing what God has given you to assist your fellow man.

Praises, praises, praises show ghastly Satan we are winning.
Keep those accolades coming right from the very beginning.

To God be the glory for all He has done,
Give our praises to Him and the battles will be won.

BIRTHDAYS

Birthdays are special because birthdays are from God!

Birthdays are to be acknowledged and celebrated!

Birthdays are to be appreciated, each individually cherished!

Birthdays are to be shared with friends and family!

Birthdays are energizing, stimulating, and reviving!

Birthdays are a unique blessing just for us!

Birthdays are a blessing because we are above ground to enjoy another one.

Birthdays are fun, adventure, reminiscing, and planning!

Birthdays are to be held aloft boldly, for they provide the opportunity to move on!

Here's hoping you claimed all of the above for your birthday!

JUST A NUMBER

Well, how does it feel to be fifty-eight?
Thank God while you shout, "It's really, really great!"

A mind that is filled with magnificent thoughts,
and a heart full of thankfulness cannot be bought.

It's an age in my life when the race can slow down,
for competitors and co-workers aren't milling around.

It's a time when spiritual growth continues to expand,
when your dependence on the Bible is greater than on man.

It's a time when you look back over exigent years,
to marvel at things that caused major stress and tears.

Knees and feet, eyes and ears, don't work as well as twenty,
but life is strong and now you know health's not bought with money.

The passing years have taught me most graciously to rely,
on the Father's might power, which peace will always supply.

Thank you, thank you, thank you for the length of life You've given,
with sufficient sadness to recognize that joy makes life worth living.

So prayers to the Father are now passionate and keen,
By fifty-eight you know true life, and what it really means.

CELEBRATING SIXTY!

60…followed by multiple sets of zeros—great lottery prize

60…preceded by multiple sets of zeros—nothing but sixty

60…with a point in the middle—bad Olympic diving score

60…with a point in the middle—great Olympic skating score

60…waiting for retirement—bad because you're not there yet

60…waiting for retirement—great because the end is nearer than it has been

60…an age not to feel old—simply feel mature and knowledgeable

60…an age to enjoy "grand" little people

60…an age that depends on your own personal perspective

60…an age that allows you enough time to begin something

60…a standard measurement of time and time has been good to you

60…a time to begin to slow down so you can plan the specifics for your "golden years"

60…looking back over those sixty years may reveal:

- The struggle to keep strong family ties
- Unbelievable travel adventures
- A dedicated work ethic that has grown over the years
- A natural change in physical acuity
- A chance to look back and smile at the some of the things you
- struggled with over the years
- The opportunity to look forward to a future filled with all the goodness life can offer
- A chance to say, "Thank God."

Enjoy your 60th birthday—it is a milestone!

GREEN BLESSING

God in His infinite wisdom gave us earth,
which was complete and usable when first it was birthed.
It came with few instructions that were quickly ignored,
because man became greedy and inappropriately bored.
The rolling, green meadows, babbling brooks, ocean shores,
majestic mountains, savannas, sandy deserts, and fjords…
all of its inhabitants with each gene placed intact,
have become blurred because of man's preservation lack.
The cerulean firmament in which gentle clouds sauntered by,
now looks opaque and murky, not the once beautiful blue sky.
After millions of years, the earth is looking quite old,
because of man's ignorance of basic damage control.
Landfills and plastics, pollution and destruction,
cement and asphalt, steel and construction…
All of these things have caused problems for Mother Earth.
Man's lessened her value and minimized her worth.
God loaned us a place to live, work, and play.
He expected us to keep it in a clever, insightful way.
The picture's coming clearer; we now know what we must do—
clean up, clear up, uncover, tear down, restore, renew.
These jobs belong to everyone, in towns, cities, and countryside.

All must work to defend and protect the place where we reside.
God still helps with the wind and rain, also frosts and snow,
to keep our place very well stocked with what we need to grow.
Thank you, Father, from our hearts; we are most sincerely blessed.
We will enhance our propensity for our earth's needs to be addressed.

I AM MUSIC

I am music.

I am praises and gifts and solitude.

Written and unwritten

With or without words

Hummed, chanted, sung, thought

I give meaning to life.

Raise souls from the doldrums, express emotion,

Enlighten, change mood

I am music.

Available to any and all beings…

There are no rules.

I can be brief, creative, an utterance

Not written, never to be heard again.

As the wind passes, I can be heard and gone.

Or

I can be meticulously written for voice of instruments

Concocted with sticks, brush, or whatever is at hand.

I can be a melody that has passed through the ages,

Known by many, recognized by many, played by many

I am music.

As a word I can be defined.

But a feeling, emotion and energy, I cannot.

Praises, adorations, shouts, scriptural expressions, chants

All individualized to each unique spirit.

I am music!

RARING TO GO!

Mind packed.

Eyes focused.

Lips moistened with positives.

Heart filled with the Word.

Hands cleaned of transgressions.

Feet directed.

Soul inspired.

Spirit glowing.

Now…set.

Ready to start the day!

THE FRAGRANCE OF LOVE

A glance from softened eyes is inhaled from across the room.

No words need to be spoken.

A sachet of a smile floats effortlessly from his lips to hers.

No sounds need be heard.

The luscious sweetness of a tender touch evokes

warmth and attention without vocal utterance.

The aroma of understanding wafts between the two;

each one knowing what the other is thinking.

The gentleness of a kiss strategically placed.

The fragrance of love flows naturally between these mature lovers,

whose years of marriage have garnered respect, knowledge,

thoughtfulness,

supportiveness, and acceptance.

Two souls…one entity.

UNPARALLELED EVENT!

There is no other American holiday that can compare with Christmas. Christmas is a time of special feelings and remembrances.

It is a time of much activity, but yet a time of inner peace. It is a time of an incredible mindset that exudes a unique patience, brightness, and significant charitable considerations toward our fellow man. It is a time of love. The birth of Jesus, the Christmas season, makes our lives livable and provides the pathway to salvation. This special event emphasized, many years ago, the need for God's people to have a Saviour.

Aside from LOVE, CHRISTMAS IS PEACE! CHRISTMAS IS HOPE! CHRISTMAS IS JOY! What wonderment surrounds this season! As we remember Jesus' birth, the sentiment that fills each heart is inexplicable. Christmas is our gift. Christmas is our blessing.

We welcome the baby Jesus. We welcome our Saviour. We stand in awe of our God and His Son's season. Our future is in Him.

We thank God for the wonderful gift of memory. Let us remember the closeness and the blessings of Christmases past and listen to God's directions for today as we honor that incredible birth. Let us, in gratitude, rejoice by sharing this great gift with others through our words, our actions, and our "light."

PRAYERS AND RESPONSES

SUPPLICATIONS WITH SINCERITY!
PRAYER CHANGES THINGS!

ADVERSITY

Through glistening tears and moistened cheeks, through pursed lips and downtrodden heart, eyes lift to whisper an almost inaudible praise to God, the Father of all circumstance. Hallelujah! For in every dark moment, every devastating loss, every malevolent defeat, there is hidden an infinitesimal glimmer of an optimistic outcome

If eyes can cry, if breath can be taken to heave a sigh, if arms can be lifted toward the sky, some good can be found in grave adversity.

Praise to the Father, who is always in control.

Praise to the Father, for all He has allowed us to experience.

Praise to the Father, for how He raised us from iniquity.

We are humbled and reflective, as we await His message.

Precious Father, give us the words we need to move forward, moving the life with which you have blessed us, toward an altruistic existence for humankind.

The need for understanding lingers.

The capturing of understanding is elusive.

The implementation of understanding is complicated.

But…we know that you will provide all that is needed to continue along life's crooked path. Adversity is but a stumbling block over which you can order our steps, if we but ask. Honor and glory we extend to you with grateful hearts, even in times of adversity.

Amen.

CHRISTMAS PRAYER

Father, as we watch flickering candles, our hearts are filled with Gratitude. As we inhale the frankincense and internalize the manger Scene, we feel overwhelming gratitude for your Son, Jesus. It is amazing that you loved us so much you sent Him to us. Jesus came to give us salvation. Keep this miracle forever clear in our minds. This is the season of Jesus; a time of peace in our hearts, for our world is in such turmoil. Even so, this is a time for joy in our lives, for you have promised us joy. Christmas is a time for giving, as we mimic your actions to us and those of the wise men to baby Jesus. We can give from our hearts, which costs us nothing. Christmas is a time for loving, you first, and all others thereafter. Thank you, Father.

Christmas is special! Allow it to engulf us, as we receive, acknowledge, and accept that extraordinary blessing—Jesus Christ.

We celebrate His birth by continuing to marvel at His life, yet we remain humble, respecting the salvation purchased by His death.

Thank you, Father, for sending us the Light of our world. Let that Light fill our hearts with overflowing contentment, but let that contentment not lie dormant. Let it activate the sharing, caring, and giving of ourselves. Let us absorb the season and distribute its glowing warmth throughout the upcoming year. Grant peace, joy, and strength for the elevating of your kingdom. Amen.

CHRISTMAS WILL ALWAYS

Be Christmas

This has been a year! (2007) I'd like to paraphrase two very unlikely people for this occasion; Dr. Seuss and Pastor Rick Warren with two important points: (1) in Dr. Seuss' *The Grinch Who Stole Christmas*, all the presents were stolen from the homes in Whoville by the Grinch, and the decorations were ramshackled. Christmas, in the form of a bright, glowing light, came anyway and the Whos were overjoyed and celebrated. That was quite a revelation for the Grinch, who was trying to steal the Who's Christmas happiness. God's happiness cannot be taken from you. Point (2) Pastor Warren wrote a book called, *The Purpose of Christmas*. In a television interview (November, 2007), he reminded us that Christmas is not the office or group parties, gift buying, house decorating, or time off. It is the birthday of Jesus! Pastor Warren stated that if all of those things were gone, it would still be Christmas! He mentioned in that interview, realizing it had been a difficult year and many of us won't have or do what we usually experience during this season, remember if we have nothing…Christmas will come without any preparation. All we need is to be ready in our hearts.

We all know the story: the chosen maiden who convinced a child by the Holy Spirit, her husband-to-be, who at first rejected her, the messages from the angels, and the trek to Bethlehem because of a tax decree and the lodging chaos. We recall being told of the magnificent star, the chorus of angels, the shepherds and the wise men. All were contained in God's glorious plan and that plan changed the world as it had been known. The gifts to the baby Jesus, the adoration of the Little One, or the gratitude to the Father can never be matched or synchronized.

But think back over the year and designate one moment in your mind for which you are most grateful to God. There are probably so many that it could be difficult to choose only one. It does not have to be spoken. It is between you and God. Think on that as you offer up a prayer of thanksgiving. Then, since it is a birthday, decide what gift you can give Jesus. It is not tangible; it must come from the heart. Perhaps it could be a sincere outreach that you will execute throughout the year as your personal gift for Christmas. No monetary exchanges are needed, for we know with nothing in hand or in pockets, our sense of Christmas joy will always be there. Nothing can take that sense of joy from you.

O God, you are so awesome! You have crossed all the T's and dotted all the I's. The detail with which you have given us the Christmas story is astounding. We can hardly take it all in. You have provided the Light of the world. We symbolize that Light with candles and candlelight services. We are grateful and thankful to you, God, for all that you have done for us; a functioning mind, eyes, ears, legs, and a heart that feels and performs. If we are lacking in any area, by your grace we carry on and move forward. How great is your countenance! You gave us your Son, Jesus, to provide salvation and deliverance. And as we celebrate your Son, we want to humbly acknowledge the need for you in our lives and to specifically thank you for Jesus. Our prayer is to live our lives and execute your will with honor, praise, and glory to you. Thank you for Christmas. It is another opportunity to say, "Thank you and praise you, Father!" Amen.

DAILY PRAYER

Father God, we awaken and know that our lives are in your hands; we thank you and shout praises and hallelujahs to you, our awesome God. We await all the wonderful possibilities and blessings that you have for us this day. There are so many inviting detours along the pathway to your kingdom. We ask that we skirt the problems or that you walk with us through the detours. We pray to stay focused, and to be very conscious and knowledgeable of your Word and all that you provide for us. You, God, make our mountains movable, our troubled waters smooth, and our clouded thoughts clear. We know this day holds many opportunities to share your teachings with others, to let your light shine through us, and to uplift those subjugated by circumstance. Grant us, through our personal worship and acclamation, a deeper understanding and appreciation of your gifts to us, as we magnify and glorify your Holy Name. Amen.

PRAYER FOR LENT

Lord, we are so unworthy.

Praise, honor, and adoration we give to you.

We thank you for being our Savior and Redeemer.

We thank you, Father, for your grace and your mercy.

Lord, help us as we strive to do your will.

Mold us…make us instruments of your goodness.

Especially during the Lenten season, let us remember the anger, the intensity, and the severity of the Crucifixion of Christ.

Let us rededicate our existence to service, to being positive, and to love, understand, and appreciate the sacrifice that was made for us.

Thank you, Father, for your Son, Jesus, who followed your will…

Thank you, Father, for His obedience…

Thank you, Father, for providing our Salvation. Amen.

PRAYER FOR THANKSGIVING

I THESSALONIANS 5:18

"In everything give thanks; for this is the will of God in Christ Jesus concerning you."

Father, you hold all gifts and grace, all treasures and discovery.

Open our eyes at this time of Thanksgiving that we might behold the wonders of your love for us, your Word to us, and your world around us. Give us insight to perceive beyond these gifts to the Giver. Let us freely choose to follow you and to humbly thank you for all that you have given us through your grace. We give thanks for our families, our children, our sources of income, and our health. We give thanks for those around us. Our days are filled with gifts that we take for granted. It is not by our strategy that we are bestowed, but by your grace. We ask blessings on all state of affairs over which we have no control. Allow us to look lovingly with knowledge of you in all situations and circumstances. Know, Father, that we give thanks for your deity and your Son, Jesus. Amen.

RESPONSIVE READING ~ MUSICIANS PROVIDE WORSHIP

LEADER: Sing praises to God. Sing praises. Sing praises to our King.

Sing praises. God is the King of the earth. Sing a song of praise to him (Psalm 47: 6).

PEOPLE: Music is the echo of the heart and the sustainer of the soul. It connects all ages, tongues, and races.

LEADER: Shout with joy to God. Sing about his glory. Make his praise glorious. Sing that his works are amazing. All people should be glad and sing (Psalm 66: 1-2).

PEOPLE: Music is the echo of the heart and the sustainer of the soul. It lifts burdens, lightens weights, and offers hope.

LEADER: I will always sing of his love. I will sing unto the Lord a new song because he has done miracles. All come before the Lord with singing (Psalm 89: 1, 98: 1).

PEOPLE: Music is the echo of the heart and the sustainer of the soul. It broadens knowledge while providing a shared testimony of his goodness.

LEADER: Because of spiritual gifts, I will pray with my spirit and I will pray with my mind, I will sing with my spirit and will sing with my mind. Pray and sing! Praise ye the Lord. Sing unto the Lord a new song (1 Corinthians 14: 15; Psalm 149: 1).

PEOPLE: Music is the echo of the heart and the sustainer of the soul.

God's music takes many forms and has many purposes from which all can soothe any need.

LEADER: Bless the Lord, O my soul; And all that is within me, bless his holy name (Psalm 103: 1).

CHOIRS: I commit my voice, my words, my mind, and body to you, God. I will sing sincerely with understanding. I will strive to be cooperative, and rehearse to sing to bring all glory and praise to you. Amen.

LEADER: I am the vine, ye are the branches; He that abideth in me, and I in him, the same bringeth forth much fruit; for without me ye can do nothing (John 15: 5).

PEOPLE: Praise God! We stand to give thanks for your Son, Jesus, and we consider ourselves a blessed people for without you, we are nothing.

LEADER: And God gave him wisdom and understanding exceeding much, and largeness of heart, even as the sand that is on the sea-shore; and he spoke three thousand proverbs and his songs were a thousand and five; and all the people came to hear his wisdom (1 Kings 4: 29, 32, 34).

PEOPLE: We stand giving thanks for the gifts and wisdom planted by God in the minds of men to journey from afar and be fruitful. They gathered the wanderers and provided direction.

LEADER: And how shall they preach, except they be sent? I will send you pastors according to mine heart, which I shall feed you with knowledge and understanding (Romans 10: 15; Jeremiah 3: 15).

PEOPLE: We are thankful for the pastors God has sent to lead and nurture his congregation through these many years. We have been edified and spiritually filled.

LEADER: Every good gift and every perfect gift is from above, and cometh down from the Father of Lights, with whom is no variableness, neither shadow of turning (James 1: 17).

PEOPLE: We bless and praise you, Lord, for our gains in uplifting your kingdom and for allowing us to be a beacon through which your Light might pass.

LEADER: Now ye are the body of Christ, and members in particular.

And God hath set some in the church, first apostles, secondarily prophets, thirdly teachers, after thoseworkers of miracles, then gifts of healing, helps, governments and diversities of tongues (1 Corinthians 12: 27-28).

PEOPLE: We know you as an Awesome God, as we acknowledge the diverse ministries and outreach you seeded here in this church, which have touched so many.

LEADER: We give thanks to God always the body, making mention of it in our prayers; Remembering without ceasing the work of faith, and labor of love and patience of hope in our Lord Jesus Christ in the sight of God our Father (1 Thessalonians 1:2-3).

PEOPLE: We stand in prayer that the legacy of this body continues under your grace for future generations.

LEADER: But God has tempered the body together that there should be no schism in the body, but that the members should have the same care for one another. And whether one member suffers, all the members suffer with it; or should one member be honored, all the members rejoice with it. Now we are the body of Christ, and members in particular (1 Corinthians 12: 25-27).

ALL: We shout Hallelujah and sing praises to a mighty God, who brought us together from a fractured land, to be a protector, a spiritual guide, and to testify to his good works for a world in need.

Shout Hallelujah! Amen.

RESPONSIVE READING ~ HOPE ALWAYS

LEADER: Father, we are so grateful for all that you do for us each and every day. Some blessings, we are completely unaware of, but we thank you.

PEOPLE: Praise to you, Father, for your caring and love for your children

LEADER: Life cannot always be planned or predicted. We know that with you in our lives and our hearts, we can rise from despair and disillusionment.

PEOPLE: Glory to you, Father, for your mercy and your grace toward us.

LEADER: Be it water, wind, loss, fatigue, finance, or death, seemingly hopeless situations can be turned around in the twinkling of an eye.

The Lord will tap a healing source.

PEOPLE: Blessed be the name of the Lord. He is our salvation.

LEADER: All conditions have a reverse side. The reverse side of darkness is light...of pain is healing...of destruction is rebirth...of despair is hope.

PEOPLE: Hallelujah! Hosanna to the Lord of our lives who gives us hope!

ALL: We all must take a moment to keep the candle of hope lit for all people in need of God's assistance and peace; whether they are located on the Gulf Coast, West Coast, North Carolina, Haiti, Somalia, Afghanistan, or Iraq, anywhere across our world. Even in this very place, there are needs that require hope. We hold hands and share hugs to remind ourselves that people need each other.

May we all take the time to do our part, no matter how small, to pray, to give, or do something for someone else, knowing that God will have the final word and He will multiply the tiniest outreach for the multitude! Hope always, for without it we will perish.

Amen.

RESPONSIVE READING FOR THE MARRIAGE CEREMONY

LEADER: Marriage takes *time*. It cannot be entered into with all the necessary components to succeed. For each marriage is unique and requires specific components that relate specifically to each couple's makeup and characteristics, which are unknown at the beginning of a marital relationship.

PEOPLE: In marriage as in all things, seek God's kingdom first. Do what He asks and all things needed, will be provided to you.

LEADER: Marriage takes *patience*. Each partner feels differently, thinks differently, and acts differently during any shared moment.

Therefore, it is necessary to take the time to consider both perspectives, contemplate the total impact and then respond to the circumstances.

PEOPLE: Patience is rare quality. Hold tight to God while using patience to disseminate every situation. Decisions made and tasks completed in haste or with quick temper, cannot bring about positive resolution.

LEADER: Marriage takes *understanding*. Understanding means both partners must look from the other's perspective, which requires attentive listening without being judgmental.

PEOPLE: Listening to the Lord's teachings will make us wise. This will make a shared life happy. For the Lord decides what a person's life will be.

LEADER: Marriage takes *faithfulness*. When days are not filled with excitement and beauty, or when a relationship is experiencing stress and agreement is elusive, and money trickles; husbands and wives must remain true to each other and to their union.

PEOPLE: The naked eye observes the stresses and the lack of cohesiveness that are apparent, but the outcome and the future of a marriage are in God's domain. Seek His will.

LEADER: Marriage takes *sharing and communicating*. Both of which require *trust* that allows each partner to disclose his and her thoughts and emotions, uncover egos, and abandon defensiveness.

A God-centered union can share, communicate, and trust, knowing these delicate sensitivities will be respected and protected by the partner.

PEOPLE: God created caring hearts that possess respect, courtesy, kindness, and compassion. Armed with these attributes, the courage to converse will come. God will be the shield for those who put their trust in Him.

LEADER: Marriage is *love*. Love involves time, patience, understanding, faithfulness, sharing, communication, and trust. Love includes God as the interlocking substance that holds it all together, for it is not by human power that marriages last.

ALL: Be excited about God! Be excited about life! Be excited about each other! Be excited about marriage whether its length is one year, sixty years, or planned for next year!

RESPONSIVE READING ~ OPENING OF VACATION BIBLE SCHOOL

LEADER: They will come from high rises, single-family homes, row houses, apartments and homeless shelters. They will be tall, short, dark, light, round, and lean. Then will be of all ages. They all come with one main goal.

PEOPLE: Vacation Bible School is a time of relaxed study of God's Word through learning, fellowship, music, and crafts.

LEADER: They will come with enthusiasm and passion, eager to absorb all of the facts and information presented by dedicated, committed volunteers.

PEOPLE: Vacation Bible School is a time to delve through lessons that provide knowledge and reinforcement.

LEADER: They will come to be enlightened with the Word, learning how God wants them to live and what their interactions with others should be.

PEOPLE: Vacation Bible School is a time to think about what God has planned for us. A time when the spiritual needs of the young, the elderly, and all those in between should be considered.

LEADER: During these days or weeks, they will think on these things; things that are true, honest, and just; things that are pure, lovely, and are of good report; with virtue and praise; they will think on these things.

PEOPLE: Vacation Bible School is a time for renewal and redirection.

God has provided the plan. This time of study offers an opportunity to investigate its influence in our individual lives.

LEADER: They will be creative in the Lord and worship and praise Him through their learning. Devotion will provide them with private moments of connection with God.

ALL: We are thankful for the opportunity to study together with a relaxed approach to learning. We give God the glory for providing us with this time of togetherness in his Word. Amen.

GOD, THANK YOU

T open your eyes and see the sky is lightening,
The sun is rising.
To have the morning silence broken by the rustling leaves and gentle chirps,
The birds are awakening.
To watch nature's creatures face the dawning brightness and unfurl themselves,
The morning glories have been touched.
To feel the steady beat of a heart continuing life through a breathing body,
Gratefulness abounds!
God, Thank You!

To the reader: you have reached the end of the second Butterfly Path. Hopefully the path provided an awakening and insightful to a positive viewpoint.
May God's Grace, Mercy, Love, and Provision
Be Always with You.
Gratefully,
Carolyn Saunders Banks

Butterflies are silent, unobtrusively busy, and discreetly task-oriented. Yet they are beautiful, induce a smile, provide a warm sense of pleasure, and could be considered a messenger from God. But what then is the message? Stop! Think! Remember! Appreciate!

A butterfly should cause us to reflect. In every human encounter there is a lesson, a blessing, or an answer. There are times that a butterfly may cross one's path as a diversion to provide an extra instant for thought or a moment that eases anxiety.

Butterflies are precious and the words written within this book of verse are also treasures. Each one is a butterfly that could be your blessing. After reading On Any Given Day . . . A Butterfly Could Be A Blessing! you may forever enjoy imaginative thinking when you view a beautifully simplistic butterfly.

Carolyn Saunders Banks is a graduate of Hampton University in Virginia.

She has done post-graduate work at Temple University in Philadelphia, PA, Meredith College, and North Carolina State University, both in Raleigh, NC. She is a retired educator with twenty-nine years in classrooms in Pittsburgh, Philadelphia, and Raleigh, and fifteen of those years as a mentor to new teachers. For nine years she managed her real estate property renovation firm with her partner, Alice Kupec. For the last ten years, she and her husband, Martin, have been caregivers in their home both their moms. This active baby boomer now devotes much of her time to her first love – writing.

www.ingramcontent.com/pod-product-compliance
Lightning Source LLC
Chambersburg PA
CBHW051206120626
46547CB00013B/1228